KACY HEILIG

EMAIL MARKETING TIPS

The Complete Guide on Email Marketing Techniques, Learn
The Secrets and Tips on How You Can Build An Expensive
Mailing List That Is Guaranteed to Generate Sales

Descrierea CIP a Bibliotecii Naţionale a României
KACY HEILIG
    EMAIL MARKETING TIPS. The Complete Guide on
Email Marketing Techniques, Learn The Secrets and Tips on
How You Can Build An Expensive Mailing List That Is
Guaranteed to Generate Sales / Kacy Heilig. – Bucharest: Editura
My Ebook, 2020
    ISBN

KACY HEILIG

EMAIL MARKETING TIPS

The Complete Guide on Email Marketing Techniques, Learn The Secrets and Tips on How You Can Build An Expensive Mailing List That Is Guaranteed to Generate Sales

My Ebook Publishing House
Bucharest, 2020

TABLE OF CONTENT

INTRODUCTORY

Email marketing is quickly becoming one of the most popular forms of Internet advertising.

This is because there are many distinct advantages to the concept of email marketing. However, email marketing does have some disadvantages as well. In this article we will examine the advantages and disadvantages of email marketing and will also provide some insight into how to plan and execute an effective email marketing campaign.

Email marketing certainly has a set of unique advantages over other types of marketing both online and offline. Perhaps one of the most significant advantages to email marketing is the ability to reach a worldwide audience with minimal effort.

It is certainly possible to reach a worldwide audience with other types of advertising but traditional types of advertising such as television, radio and the print media are not nearly as effective for reaching potential customers around the world all at once.

Another major advantage to email marketing is it is extremely affordable. This is significant because there are many other types of marketing, including Internet marketing, which are significantly more expensive than email marketing.

The costs associated with email marketing are minimal. Ideally you will already have a list of email recipients who are interested in your products and services so there is no cost associated with obtaining a list of email addresses. Additionally, the cost to send out emails is minimal and can be considered part of your regular operating costs. All of these factors already make email marketing extremely cost effective.

However, there is some cost involved in email marketing. Primarily this is the costs associated with writing the advertisements and creating any graphics which will accompany the email advertisements. This will require hiring a writer to write the copy for the advertisement and a designer to create and implements the graphics. The cost of these services will vary pretty widely but in general you will pay more for writers and designers with more experience. This is because these writers and designers are expected to be able to produce a higher quality of work than those with less experience could produce.

The most obvious disadvantage to email marketing is the possibility of having your email marketing viewed as spam. This is a very important problem because it could prove to be quite costly in terms of the profit margin for your business. Each day Internet users are bombarded with unsolicited emails serving as advertisements.

This problem has reached epic proportions and the abundance of spam infiltrating the email boxes of innocent Internet users has to be cautious and suspicious about any email they receive which is unsolicited and appears to be promoting a particular product or service.

Emails which contain subject lines or content which appear to be similar to spam may be automatically transferred to a spam email folder by the email system. Emails which are not automatically deleted may be deleted without being opened simply because the recipient does not recognize the sender of the email.

Both of these problems can result in essentially wasted time for the business owner because the recipients are not even viewing the emails advertising the products and services offered by the business. Additionally, they may result in complaints being lodged against the company for being a purveyor of spam.

Now that you understand the advantages and disadvantages of email marketing, you might wonder how you can maximize the advantages to use email marketing to your advantage. The most important factor to consider is your email distribution list. This should consist of former customers who have expressed a desire to receive emails with information and advertisements as well as potential customers who have also expressed interest in more information.

The content of the emails should also be carefully considered. They should certainly highlight the products and services you offer but should do so without appearing to be a hard sales pitch.

A writer with experience in writing this type of copy should be able to assist you in providing insightful and accurate copy which also entices the reader to find out more about your products and services. Finally, your emails should provide the readers with a call to action. This should be a statement urging the reader to take a specific action such as making a purchase or researching a product.

CHAPTER 1

ADVERTISE, DO NOT SPAM

There is a fine line between advertising and spam and unfortunately many business owners do not understand the difference between the two.

This is important because while a cleaver, well planted Internet marketing campaign can help to attract new customers and keep existing customers loyal, spam is likely to alienate both new customers and existing customers.

This can be extremely damaging to profit margins for the business owners. This article will take a look at a few basic Internet marketing strategies such as banner ads, email campaign and message board posts and describe how each can quickly cross the line from cleaver advertising to spam.

Banner ads are one of the most popular strategies which accompany an Internet marketing plan. These ads are usually ads which appear at the top of websites and span the width of the website. It is from this appearance that they earned the name banner ads but actually banner ads can refer to ads of a variety of different sizes and shapes which appear in an array of different locations on a website.

In many cases the business owner purchases advertising space on these websites but the banner ad may also be placed as part of an exchange or an affiliate marketing campaign. Banner ad exchanges are situations in which one business owner posts a banner ad on his website in exchange for another business owner posting his banner ad on the other website.

These agreements may be made individually between business owners with complementary businesses or as part of exchanges facilitated by a third party. In the case of affiliate marketing, an affiliate posts and advertisement for your business in exchange for compensation when the banner ad produces a desired effect such as generating website traffic or generating a sale.

The terms of these agreements are determined beforehand and are generally based on a scale of pay per impression, pay per click or pay per sale or lead.

Now that you understand what banner ads are, it is also important to understand how they can be overused and appear to be spam. Judiciously placing your banner ad on a few websites which are likely to attract an audience similar to your target audience is smart marketing, placing your banner ad on any website which will display the ad regardless of the target audience can be construed as spam.

Internet users who feel as though your banner ads are everywhere they turn will not likely take your business seriously and are not likely to purchase products or services from you as a result of your banner ads.

Email campaigns can also be very useful tools in the industry of Internet marketing. These campaigns may involve sending periodic e-newsletters filled with information as well as advertisements, short, informative email courses or emails offering discounts on products and services.

Loyal customers who opt into your email list will likely not view these emails as spam and may purchase additional products and services from your business as a result of this marketing strategy. Additionally, potential customers who have specifically requested additional information on your products and services will also find this type of marketing to be useful.

However, email recipients who did not request information are likely to view your emails as spam. Harvesting email addresses in a deceptive manner and using these addresses to send out mass emails will likely always be considered to be spam.

Finally, message boards provide an excellent opportunity for business owners to obtain some free advertising where it will be noticed by members of the target audience. If the products and services you offer appeal to a specific niche, it is worthwhile to join message boards and online forums related to your industry of choice.

Here you will find a large population of Internet users who may have an interest in your products. You might consider including a link to your business in your signature or posting the link when it is applicable to the conversation.

However, care should be taken to carefully review the message board guidelines to ensure you are not doing anything inappropriate. This technique is smart marketing. Conversely, replying to every message with a link to your website when it is not relevant to the conversation is likely to be construed as spam by other members. Once they begin to view your posts as spam, they are not likely to visit your website via the links you post.

CHAPTER 2

CREATING EMAIL LISTS
FOR MARKETING CAMPAIGNS

If you plan to do some Internet marketing to promote your business endeavor, you should seriously consider email marketing as at least one tier of your Internet marketing campaign.

Many business owners shy away from email marketing because they believe all email marketing campaigns are purely spam. However, this is not true and not partaking in this type of marketing can cause your business to lose out on a great deal of business.

By not appealing to potential customers via email, your business may lose a great deal of business to competitors who are using email marketing campaigns to reach customers around the world. However, the first step of an email marketing campaign should be creating an email distribution list.

This article will discuss some popular options for doing this and should help to the reader to learn more about what is acceptable and what is not when it comes to email marketing.

Once you have made the decision to start using email marketing to promote your business you are likely facing the dilemma of compiling an email distribution list. This is essentially a list of email addresses to which you will email your advertising and promotional materials. One common way to gain a list of email addresses is to purchase a list from distributors.

However, this method is not very effective at all and we do not recommend it. The problem with purchasing an email list if you have no way of knowing whether or not the members of the list would have any interest at all in your products or services. This is very important because while you want to reach a large audience with your email marketing you also want this audience to be members of your overall target audience.

When you purchase an email list you may be sending your email messages to some users who might be interested but this is largely coincidental and is not likely to be well received because the message was not solicited.

Internet users are very quick to delete materials they believe to be spam without even opening or reading the emails. In fact, some Internet service providers include spam filters which may automatically delete your emails if your messages are deemed to be spam. These filters run complex algorithms on the subject heading and content of the message to determine whether or not it is spam and are quite adept at weeding out spam.

Therefore, you run the risk of having your email marketing effort turn out to be a complete waste if the majority of recipients never even read or receive the message.

A far better way to create an email distribution list for your email marketing campaign is to ask current customers as well as interested potential customers to register with your website to receive additional information and periodic updates about your products and services as well as other information which might be of interest to them.

This provides you with a database of email addresses from current customers as well as potential customers who have a genuine interest in your products and services and who are interested in learning more about these products and services.

Once you have a list of interested customers or potential customers you can send emails or create e-newsletter for distribution to the members of your email list. These documents should contain a wealth of valuable information as well as a soft sell pitch for your products and services.

This information will be valued by the readers and may help to persuade them to try your products and services. You might also want to include useful links to either your website as well as other websites which may be of interest to your readers. Your content should also contain a portion which urges the reader to take a specific action such as making a purchase or at least investigating a product further.

CHAPTER 3

UNDERSTANDING EMAIL MARKETING

Do you understand email marketing? If you do not, you do not have to worry just yet.

This is because the concept of email marketing is relatively new and many business owners have not started to take advantage of this wonderful marketing tool yet. However, there are some savvy business owners who are already employing email marketing techniques to create additional business for themselves and to gain an advantage over the competition.

While not having a great deal of knowledge about email marketing is not an immediate threat to your business, you should start learning about this concept to ensure it does not become a problem for you later as more and more business owners in your niche begin to take advantage of the concept of email marketing. This article will provide information on email marketing which should be useful to business owners who do not have experience with the subject matter.

Business owners should first understand the options available to them in terms of email marketing. The most common options include sending out mass emails with promotional materials, publishing and distributing e- newsletters and offering correspondence courses via email. The advantage to all of these marketing strategies is the ability to reach a worldwide audience.

Unlike traditional methods of marketing such as television and radio ads or print media ads which only reach an audience in a limited area anyone with access to the Internet can benefit from your email marketing techniques.

Mass emails are the most popular form of email marketing. This includes emails which are sent to hundreds, thousands or even millions of recipients at once. The problem with this type of marketing is the potential for having your emails viewed as spam. This is likely to occur if you send your emails to recipients who have no interest in your products or services and have not expressed interest in receiving emails from you.

E-newsletters are also becoming increasingly popular as a form of email marketing. E-newsletters can be a simple or as complex as you prefer and may include text, graphics, advertisements, links or any combination of these elements.

One of the first decisions you will have to make is whether you wish to make your e-newsletter strictly text or include graphics in the e-newsletter. If you are on a tight budget, it may be worthwhile to only include text to avoid the need to hire a graphic artist. You may be able to incorporate graphics yourself but they won't look nearly as professional as the graphics provided by a professional.

Likewise, you can certainly write your own copy for your e-newsletter but you will likely create a much better impression if you hire a qualified professional writer to create the content for you instead.

Hiring a professional graphic artist and a professional writer may seem like an extraneous expense but it is actually quite important. Your e-newsletter may be the first impression many potential customers get of you and your work so it is important to make sure everything is of the highest quality.

Correspondence courses offered via email is the final email marketing strategy we will discuss. These courses may be either offered for a fee and turn into a source of income themselves or they may be made available for free.

The theory behind offering these courses for free is they often contain subtle advertising urging visitors to invest in the products and services offered by your business. Whether you charge for your email correspondences courses or offer them for free, care should be taken to ensure the information contained in these courses is completely accurate.

This is critical because potential customers who receive these email courses will be judging your business based on the quality and accuracy of these email courses. If they are filled with errors the potential customer may doubt the quality of your work and seek out the products and services offered by others including your direct competitors.

CHAPTER 4

WHY NOT EMAIL MARKETING?

If you are currently participating in other types of Internet marketing but not email marketing you should seriously consider why you are avoiding this type of advertising.

This is important because email marketing can be a very important part of an Internet marketing campaign. Many business owners avoid email marketing for fear of being accused of spamming. Internet markets may not have a clear understanding of what is spam and what is not so they avoid participation in email marketing campaigns to avoid the potential for being labeled a spammer.

Why are Internet marketers so afraid of being accused of being purveyors of spam? This is a common fear for a number of reasons. First of all, there may be harsh penalties associated

24

with sending spam emails. Recipients of spam have the option of reporting the spam to their Internet service provider who will investigate the validity of the claim. If the originator of the email is determined to be a spammer there can be harsh consequences.

Internet marketers are also afraid of email marketing because they believe it will not be well received by potential customers. This is an important concept because Internet users are bombarded with spam each day. Receiving this quantity of spam each day can be frustrating and can anger some Internet users.

These Internet users are not likely to be receptive to email marketing. The fear that these potential customers will view email marketing and stray to competitors keeps many Internet marketers from taking advantage of this type of marketing strategy.

However, it is important to note that despite the prevalent problem with spam, many Internet users are quite receptive to email marketing. This is especially true in situations where they specifically requested to receive more information from the business owner regarding his products and services.

Potential clients are particularly receptive to email marketing which provides something of value to the recipient of the email. Emails which contain in depth articles, useful tips or product reviews may be appreciated by consumers.

Additionally, items such as e-newsletters and correspondence courses offered via email can be of particular interest to potential customers. E- newsletters are typically longer documents than traditional email marketing pieces and can provide a great deal of additional information to the email recipient.

Email correspondence courses may be offered in short segments and typically amount to a significant amount of information which is likely to be greatly appreciated by the email recipients.

One final way to prevent email recipients from viewing your email marketing efforts as spam is to only send the emails to recipients who register with your website and specifically request for you to send them additional information and promotional materials. This opt in formula is ideal because it ensures you are not wasting your email marketing efforts on recipients who are not interested in your products or services.

It also ensures the recipients of the email marketing campaign do not view the informative and promotional materials they are receiving as spam. This technique for compiling an email distribution list is quite effective but it is important to remember you should always include information on how recipients can opt out of receiving future emails, www.Automatic- Responder.com is a great service to help with this.

This is important because the email recipients may have once been interested in receiving marketing emails but over time this may change. If they are no longer interested in these emails, they may begin to view the emails as spam if they are not given the option of being removed from the distribution list.

CHAPTER 5

THE REACTION TO YOUR EMAIL MARKETING

Email marketing can actually be much more effective than most people think. Many business owners do not invest a great deal of time, energy or money into orchestrating an email marketing campaign because they mistakenly believe all email marketing is viewed as spam. However, this is simply not true.

Business owners who have discovered how to market via email successfully, enjoy a great deal of success with this type of marketing. This article will discuss how email marketing can be successful and will provide insight into how to determine how your email marketing is being received.

Before we can discuss how to determine the reaction to your email marketing campaign, it is important for business owners to understand how to plan and execute an email marketing campaign which is successful.

Perhaps one of the most important elements of type of campaign is to ensure your marketing efforts are not viewed by the recipients as being spam.

One way to do this is to carefully develop your email distribution list. Although you can reach a tremendous audience by sending out your email marketing materials to a large email list, this is not effective when you do not know much about whether or not the members of this email list will even be interested in your products or services. It is important to note that reaching a huge audience is not more important than reaching a highly targeted audience.

Focusing your email marketing efforts on millions of recipients who do not have a specific interest in your products or services is not nearly as effective focusing your email marketing efforts on only hundreds of email recipients who are likely to be very interested in your products or services. This is because you are much more likely to generate sales from a small, target group than you are from a large group without a specific focus.

Now that you know a little bit about email marketing and how it can be effective, you might wonder how you can determine just how effective your email marketing efforts are in the long run. This is important because it is not worthwhile to invest a great deal of time, energy and money into an email marketing campaign if your efforts are not generating results.

Likewise, if your email marketing campaign is widely successful, you might want to consider organizing additional marketing efforts to further your success. We recommend www.Automatic-Responder.com if you do not already have an autoresponder service.

Customer surveys are one of the easiest ways to evaluate the reaction to your email marketing campaign. Asking customer to fill out simple surveys when they make a purchase can provide a great deal of insight depending on the questions you ask. Questions such as where the customer learned about your products and services may seem rather innocuous but this information can actually be rather useful to the business owner.

Learning where a customer learned about the products and services you offer, provides excellent feedback for which of your marketing efforts are generating the most interest. If you receive a great deal of responses stating customers learned about your products or services through emails, this is a good indication that your email marketing campaign is effective.

Another very popular way to evaluate the reaction to your email marketing efforts is to closely monitor your rate of sales as well as your website traffic immediately after you issue a new email to members of your distribution list. This can be helpful because an increase in sales or website traffic after an email was issued is a strong indication that the email was well received and encouraged recipients to visit the website and make purchases.

However, there is one caveat to this method of evaluation. It can be quite difficult to determine whether or not the emails caused the increase in website traffic and sales if more than one marketing effort was made at the same time. For example, if you issue an email at the same time as you launch a banner ad, you cannot determine which one is more effective and is driving the increase in sales and traffic.

CHAPTER 6

EMAIL MARKETING STRATEGIES

Email marketing is becoming extremely popular but this does not mean all business owners know how to run an effective email marketing campaign.

However, those who are well versed in the subject of email marketing and have experiencing using popular strategies effectively are likely to gain a huge advantage over their competitors who do not have these skills. This article will provide useful information for business owners who are hoping to improve their sales or website traffic through effective email marketing.

If you do not have a great deal of information about email marketing and do not fully understand the principals involved one of the best ways to orchestrate a truly effective email marketing campaign is to hire a consulting firm with a proven track record in promoting business through email marketing to assist you in your endeavor.

Similarly, to traditional marketing such as radio, television and print media, the popular strategies governing email marketing are changing constantly. As a business owner you likely already have enough to deal with trying to stay up to date on business practices that you do not have the time, energy or finances to also stay up to date on the latest changes in email marketing.

For this reason, it is certainly worthwhile to hire a professional in the email marketing industry who can devote himself full time to keeping up to date with the most effective email marketing strategies and designing an email marketing campaign for our business to help you achieve your business-related goals.

However, selecting a consultant from the many options available can be downright overwhelming. In general, you should look for a consultant who has a great deal of experience, a proven track record, listens to your questions carefully, explains concepts simply and makes your project a priority.

Another popular strategy for email marketing is to offer an email correspondence course on a subject closely related to your website or the products or services you offer. These correspondence courses should include a number of short segments, provide useful information, be of interest to your intended audience and should also help to promote your business in some way. The simplest way to promote your business without having your correspondence course deemed to be spam is to use a soft sell approach to subtly urge readers to make a purchase or visit your website for more information.

Publishing and distributing period e-newsletters is another example of an email marketing strategy which can be highly effective. An e-newsletter is very similar to a newsletter which is printed and distributed by conventional methods such as mail delivery.

The bulk of an e-newsletter should be quality content in the form of featured articles, short articles containing useful tips or product reviews. The e- newsletter may also contain graphical elements. These elements may simply be graphic designs or they may be graphics which also serve as links. The links may direct traffic to your website or to other websites. Finally, your e-newsletters should contain some type of soft sell sales approach.

It is important to not make the sales pitch blatant as this may result in the e-newsletter being considered spam. Finally, the e-newsletter should contain a call to action urging the readers to either make a purchase or visit your website for more information.

Regardless of the method of email marketing you opt to utilize, one of the most important strategies is to evaluate the effectiveness of your email marketing on a regular basis. This is critical because elements of your email marketing campaign which are not working should be weeded out. Likewise, elements of your marketing campaign which are enjoying a high degree of success should be utilized more often.

For example, if you notice there is a spike in sales or website traffic each time you issue an e-newsletter, it might be worthwhile to begin issuing e- newsletters more often. This type of evaluation and feedback can turn a moderate success into a huge success.

CHAPTER 7

IS YOUR EMAIL MARKETING SPAM?

Email marketing can be very effective as long as it is not viewed as spam.

This is critical because when your email marketing is viewed as spam, it will not likely be read by the recipient and may not even reach the recipient if it is trapped by the Internet service providers spam filter.

For this reason, it is critical for business owners to work hard to ensure the email marketing they use is not viewed as spam by either the recipient or the recipient's Internet service provider. This article will take a look at email marketing and specifically how business owners can ensure their emails are not viewed as spam.

The distribution list for an email marketing campaign is one of the critical elements which can help to ensure the emails sent by the business owner are not viewed as spam. Before this can be accomplished it is important to understand exactly what spam is.

Spam is essentially email which is unsolicited and sent for the sole purpose of advertising or promoting a product or service. Internet users receive mass quantities of spam on a daily basis. For some Internet users this quantity of spam is a huge source of frustration.

Other Internet users have become so used to the amount of spam they receive that they barely even notice these emails. Neither of these scenarios bode well for business owners who are using email marketing campaigns to promote their products or services. Internet users who are angered by these spam emails may react harshly and report your emails to their Internet service providers.

Internet users who do not even notice spam are likely to either automatically delete your emails and may block your email address to prevent future emails from getting through to them.

Paying special attention to your email distribution list and only including recipients who had specifically asked for additional information will help to keep your emails from being viewed as spam. One way to acquire email addresses for the purposes of orchestrating an email campaign is to ask interested customers to register with your website and specify whether or not they wish to receive future emails with additional information, advertisements or other useful tips.

This ensures the recipients of your emails are genuinely interested in your products and services and are not likely to view your emails as spam.

Another way to ensure your emails are not viewed as spam is to offer recipients the option of being removed from the distribution list with each email. This is important even when the recipients specifically asked to receive these emails because they are entitled to change their opinion at any time.

Offering the email recipients, the opportunity to remove themselves from the email distribution list whenever they want is worthwhile because it allows recipients to have some control in the situation. This is a stark contrast to spam in which the recipients feel as though they have no control over the situation and no way to stop the spam from bombarding their inboxes on a daily basis.

Finally, business owners can help to ensure their email marketing campaign is not viewed as spam by including quality content in the emails they send to the recipients on the email distribution list. This may include providing feature articles, product reviews or a series of short useful tips which will likely be of interest to all who receive these emails.

These emails may also include a soft sales pitch but this sales pitch should not be the focus of the emails. Putting too much attention on the advertising is likely to lead the recipients to assume the email is nothing more than spam.

Conversely, providing quality information which is useful to the recipient and subtly urging them to perform an action such as making a purchase or investigating the details of a product can make the email seem much more worthwhile and less like spam.

Printed by Libri Plureos GmbH in Hamburg,
Germany

.